Google Sites

FOR BEGINNERS

GOOGLE SITES FOR BEGINNERS

The Complete Step-By-Step Guide On How To Create A Website, Exhibit Your Team's Work, And Collaborate Effectively

While every precaution has been taken in the preparation of this book, the publisher assumes no responsibility for errors or omissions, or for damages resulting from the use of the information contained herein.

GOOGLE SITES FOR BEGINNERS: THE COMPLETE STEP-BY-STEP GUIDE ON HOW TO CREATE A WEBSITE, EXHIBIT YOUR TEAM'S WORK, AND COLLABORATE EFFECTIVELY

First edition. November 28, 2023.

Copyright © 2023 Voltaire Lumiere.

Written by Voltaire Lumiere.

TABLE OF CONTENTS

CHAPTER 1

INTRODUCTION TO GOOGLE SITES

- **Basics of Google Sites: Understanding the fundamentals.**

Google Sites is a user-friendly web design platform that enables individuals and businesses to create websites effortlessly. At its core, Google Sites operates on the principle of simplicity, allowing users to build a web presence without the need for extensive coding or technical expertise.

Upon entering the Google Sites environment, users are greeted by an intuitive interface that seamlessly integrates with other Google Workspace applications. The platform is designed to streamline the website creation process, making it accessible to both beginners and experienced users.

One of the key features defining the basics of Google Sites is its template system. Users can choose from a variety of templates tailored to different purposes, including portfolios, project showcases, and informational sites. These templates serve as a foundation, providing a structured layout that users can customize according to their specific needs.

The page creation process involves a straightforward approach. Users can add and edit text, insert images, and embed multimedia elements effortlessly. The drag-and-drop functionality simplifies the placement of content, allowing for a dynamic and visually appealing presentation.

Collaboration lies at the heart of Google Sites, allowing multiple users to work on a site simultaneously. Real-time editing capabilities ensure that changes are instantly reflected, fostering seamless teamwork.

As users delve into the basics, they discover the significance of navigation in structuring their sites. Google Sites offers an easy-to-use system for organizing pages and subpages, allowing for an intuitive and user-friendly experience for visitors.

In essence, grasping the basics of Google Sites is about recognizing its user-centric design, templated approach, collaborative features, and the simplicity it brings to website creation. As users navigate through these fundamental aspects, they gain the foundation needed to explore the platform's more advanced capabilities.

- **Advantages of Google Sites: Exploring the benefits.**

1. effective solution for website creation. Users with a Google account can access the platform at no additional cost, eliminating the need for expensive subscriptions or hosting fees. This advantage makes it an attractive option for individuals and small businesses with budget constraints.

2. **Real-Time Collaboration:** Collaboration is elevated to a new level with Google Sites. Multiple users can collaborate on the same site simultaneously, with changes reflecting in real-time. This feature is particularly advantageous for teams working on projects, as it streamlines communication and ensures everyone is on the same page.

3. **Mobile Responsiveness:** In an era where mobile devices play a crucial role in accessing information, Google Sites ensures mobile responsiveness. Websites created on the platform automatically adapt to various screen sizes, providing a consistent and optimized experience for users across desktops, tablets, and smartphones.

4. **Template Variety:** Google Sites offers a diverse range of templates catering to different purposes. Whether creating a personal portfolio, a project showcase, or an informational site, users can choose a template that aligns with their goals. This variety simplifies the initial setup process and provides a foundation for customization.

5. **Security and Reliability:** Leveraging Google's robust security measures, Google Sites ensures the safety of user data and the reliability of websites hosted on the platform. The integration with Google's infrastructure adds an extra layer of protection, making it a secure environment for website hosting.

Exploring these advantages provides a comprehensive understanding of why Google Sites is a favored platform for individuals and organizations seeking a hassle-free and feature-rich solution for website creation.

- **Key Features Overview: A glance at essential functionalities.**

Google Sites boasts a suite of key features that collectively contribute to its popularity as a user-friendly and versatile web design platform. Here's a succinct overview of the essential functionalities that define Google Sites:

1. **Intuitive Drag-and-Drop Interface:**

- The hallmark of Google Sites is its intuitive drag-and-drop interface. Users can easily add, edit, and arrange elements on their web pages without the need for complex coding or design skills.

2. **Template System for Quick Start:**

- Google Sites offers a variety of templates tailored to different purposes. Users can kickstart their website creation process by selecting a template that aligns with their goals, providing a structured foundation for customization.

3. **Seamless Integration with Google Workspace:**

- An integration powerhouse, Google Sites seamlessly incorporates files and content from other Google Workspace applications. Users can embed Google Docs, Sheets, Slides, and more directly into their sites, fostering collaboration and content diversity.

4. **Real-Time Collaboration:**

- Facilitating teamwork, Google Sites enables real-time collaboration. Multiple users can edit the same site simultaneously, ensuring that changes are instantly visible. This feature is particularly valuable for projects requiring input from various team members.

5. **Mobile Responsiveness:**

- In response to the mobile-centric era, Google Sites ensures that websites created on the platform are inherently mobile-responsive. This adaptability across different devices ensures a consistent and user-friendly experience for visitors.

6. **Versatile Content Embedding:**

- Users can enrich their sites by embedding various types of content, including images, videos, Google Maps, and more. This versatility allows for the creation of engaging and multimedia-rich web pages.

7. Customizable Design Elements:

• Google Sites provides users with the flexibility to customize design elements such as colors, fonts, and layouts. This level of customization ensures that websites can align with individual preferences and branding requirements.

8. User-Friendly Navigation System:

• The platform incorporates an easy-to-use navigation system, allowing users to organize pages and subpages efficiently. This feature contributes to an intuitive and user-friendly browsing experience for site visitors.

9. Built-in Access and Permissions Settings:

• Google Sites simplifies access management with built-in settings for user permissions. Site owners can control who can view and edit their content, ensuring privacy and security.

10. Template Customization and Advanced Features:

• While templates provide a starting point, Google Sites also allows users to customize layouts further. Advanced features, such as embedding external tools and optimizing for search engines, provide room for more sophisticated website development.

This key features overview encapsulates the essential functionalities that make Google Sites a dynamic and accessible platform for individuals and businesses alike.

- **Google Sites for Beginners: Why it's a suitable choice.**

For beginners venturing into the realm of website creation, Google Sites emerges as an ideal platform, offering a host of features and advantages that make the learning curve manageable and the overall experience enjoyable. Here's why Google Sites is a fitting choice for beginners:

1. **User-Friendly Interface:**

- Google Sites boasts an intuitive and user-friendly interface, making it accessible for individuals with varying levels of technical expertise. The platform's straightforward design empowers beginners to navigate and build websites with ease.

2. **No Coding Required:**

- Unlike some web development platforms that demand coding proficiency, Google Sites eliminates this barrier for beginners. The platform operates on a no-code principle, allowing users to create compelling websites without delving into complex programming languages.

3. **Template-Based Approach:**

- Google Sites simplifies the initial stages of website creation by offering a range of templates designed for different purposes. This template-based approach provides beginners with a structured starting point, helping them visualize and organize content effectively.

4. **Seamless Integration with Google Workspace:**

• As part of the broader Google ecosystem, Google Sites seamlessly integrates with other Google Workspace applications. This integration simplifies the process of embedding documents, spreadsheets, presentations, and other content, enhancing the overall user experience.

5. **Real-Time Collaboration:**

• Collaboration is a key strength of Google Sites, especially beneficial for beginners working on projects with others. Real-time editing features allow multiple users to contribute simultaneously, fostering teamwork and collective creativity.

6. **Mobile Responsiveness:**

• Recognizing the prevalence of mobile devices, Google Sites ensures that websites created on the platform are inherently responsive. This means that beginners can design websites that look great and function well across a variety of devices without additional effort.

7. **Cost-Effective Solution:**

• Affordability is a significant advantage for beginners, and Google Sites addresses this by offering a cost-effective solution. Users with a Google account can access the platform at no additional cost, providing a budget-friendly option for those starting their online journey.

8. **Step-by-Step Guidance:**

- Google Sites provides step-by-step guidance within its interface, offering tooltips and prompts to assist beginners in understanding various features. This on-the-go assistance ensures that users can explore and implement functionalities without feeling overwhelmed.

9. **Versatile Content Embedding:**

- Beginners can easily enrich their websites by embedding various types of content, such as images, videos, and maps. This versatility allows for the creation of visually engaging and dynamic web pages without the need for advanced design skills.

10. **Security and Reliability:**

- As part of the Google infrastructure, Google Sites ensures the security and reliability of hosted websites. Beginners can focus on content creation without concerns about data safety, trusting in the robust security measures provided by Google.

In essence, Google Sites caters to beginners by combining simplicity, accessibility, and functionality. The platform's emphasis on user-friendliness, collaboration, and integration with other

Google tools makes it an ideal choice for those taking their first steps into the world of website creation.

- **Account Setup: Step-by-step guide to creating an account.**

Creating a Google Sites account is a straightforward process that allows users to access the platform for website creation and collaboration. Follow this step-by-step guide to set up your Google Sites account:

1. **Access Google Sites:**

- Open your web browser and navigate to Google Sites by entering "sites.google.com" in the address bar.

2. **Sign In or Create a Google Account:**

- If you already have a Google account, click on "Sign In" and enter your existing credentials. If you don't have an account, click on "Create account" and follow the prompts to set up a new Google account.

3. **Google Account Information:**

- Complete the required fields, including your first and last name, desired email address (which will serve as your username), and a secure password. Follow the on-screen instructions to verify your identity and agree to Google's terms of service and privacy policy.

4. **Verify Your Account:**

•   Google may ask you to verify your identity through a phone number or an alternative email address. Follow the verification process to ensure the security of your account.

5. **Accessing Google Sites:**

•   Once your account is set up and verified, go back to "sites.google.com" and click on "Sign In." Enter the credentials for the Google account you just created or signed into.

6. **Navigate to Google Sites Dashboard:**

•   After signing in, you'll be redirected to the Google Sites dashboard. Here, you can see existing sites (if any) and start creating a new one by clicking on the "+" icon or the "Blank" template, depending on your preference.

7. **Choosing a Template (Optional):**

•   Google Sites offers various templates based on different purposes. You can choose a template to get started or opt for a blank template to build your site from scratch.

8. **Site Name and URL:**

- Give your site a name and a unique URL. The URL is part of the web address where your site will be accessible (e.g., yoursiteName.google.com). Ensure that the site name and URL are reflective of your content or purpose.

9. **Creating Your Site:**

- Once you've configured the basic settings, click on "Create" or a similar option to initiate the site creation process. You'll be directed to the editing interface, where you can start adding content, customizing the layout, and building your site.

10. **Exploring Features:**

- Familiarize yourself with the various features available, such as adding pages, inserting text and media, customizing the design, and collaborating with others in real-time.

Congratulations! You've successfully set up your Google Sites account and initiated the creation of your first website. Take your time to explore the features and unleash the potential of Google Sites for your online presence.

CHAPTER 2

PLANNING YOUR WEBSITE

- **Define Purpose and Goals: Clarifying the website's mission.**

Defining the purpose and goals of your website is a crucial first step in creating a meaningful online presence. This process involves clarifying the mission and intentions behind your website, providing a clear direction for content creation and user engagement. Here's a guide to help you define the purpose and goals of your website:

1. **Identify the Core Purpose:**

- Start by articulating the fundamental reason for creating the website. Ask yourself: What primary purpose does the website serve? Whether it's to showcase your portfolio, promote a business, share information, or engage with a community, identify the core essence of your website.

2. **Determine Target Audience:**

- Who are you creating the website for? Define your target audience by considering factors such as age, interests, demographics, and preferences. Understanding your audience will guide the content and design choices that resonate with them.

3. **Set Clear Objectives:**

- Establish specific and measurable goals for your website. These objectives could include increasing brand awareness, driving traffic, generating leads, selling products, or fostering community engagement. Clear goals provide a framework for evaluating the success of your website.

4. **Understand User Needs:**

- Consider the needs and expectations of your target audience. What information or solutions are they seeking? How can your website address their pain points or interests? Aligning your content with user needs enhances the relevance and value of your website.

5. **Define Unique Selling Proposition (USP):**

- Identify what sets your website apart from others in your niche. Define your unique selling proposition — the distinctive features, services, or content that make your website compelling and attractive to visitors.

6. **Craft a Mission Statement:**

- Summarize the purpose and goals of your website in a concise mission statement. This statement should encapsulate the essence of your website's mission, providing a guiding principle for all your content and actions.

7. **Consider Branding Elements:**

•   If your website represents a personal brand or business, think about the branding elements that convey your identity. This includes the logo, color scheme, and visual style. Consistent branding fosters recognition and reinforces the identity of your website.

8. **Outline Content Strategy:**

•   Develop a content strategy aligned with your purpose and goals. Outline the types of content you'll create, the frequency of updates, and the platforms you'll use. This strategy ensures that your content contributes meaningfully to achieving your objectives.

9. **Evaluate Monetization Options (if applicable):**

•   If your website has monetization goals, explore potential revenue streams such as advertising, affiliate marketing, or selling products/services. Ensure that your monetization strategy aligns with the overall purpose of your website.

10. **Review and Refine:**

•   Periodically review and refine your website's purpose and goals. As your brand evolves or market conditions change, ensure that your website's mission remains relevant and impactful. Regular evaluations help you stay aligned with your objectives.

By going through this process, you'll gain a comprehensive understanding of your website's mission and goals. This clarity serves as a foundation for creating content, designing user experiences, and measuring the success of your online venture.

- **Structuring Content: Organizing pages and navigation.**

Organizing the content on your website is a critical aspect of creating a positive user experience. Effectively structuring your content involves thoughtful planning of pages and navigation to ensure that visitors can easily find and engage with the information you provide. Here's a guide to help you organize your website's content:

1. **Identify Key Topics or Sections:**

- Begin by identifying the main topics or sections that your website will cover. These could be overarching themes related to your mission and goals. For example, if you have a business website, topics might include "Products," "Services," and "About Us."

2. **Create a Hierarchy of Information:**

- Establish a hierarchical structure for your content. Consider the relationships between different topics and how they fit into the overall narrative of your website. This hierarchy will guide the organization of pages and subpages.

3. Home Page Overview:

- The home page serves as the gateway to your website. Provide a concise overview of the key sections and direct visitors to the most important information. Use visually engaging elements and brief descriptions to capture attention.

4. Primary Navigation Menu:

- Design a clear and intuitive primary navigation menu. This menu typically appears at the top of your website and includes links to the main sections or pages. Ensure that it reflects the key topics identified earlier and is easy to navigate.

5. Secondary Navigation or Footer:

- Consider incorporating secondary navigation menus or a footer menu for additional pages or information. This is particularly useful if you have a large amount of content. Keep secondary menus organized and relevant to specific areas of interest.

6. Logical Page Order:

- Arrange pages in a logical order within each section. For example, on a "Products" page, the order might follow the sequence of product categories or features. Logical order enhances the flow of information and aids in user understanding.

7. Use Descriptive Page Titles:

- Craft clear and descriptive titles for each page. Page titles should provide a glimpse of the content and help visitors understand what to expect. Descriptive titles also contribute to search engine optimization (SEO).

8. Incorporate Subpages for Detail:

- If a topic requires more detailed information, create subpages to delve into specific aspects. Subpages help maintain a clean and organized layout while allowing for comprehensive coverage of your content.

9. Implement Breadcrumbs:

- Breadcrumbs are a navigational aid that displays the path a user has taken to arrive at a particular page. Implementing breadcrumbs helps visitors understand the structure of your website and easily navigate back to previous levels.

10. Mobile-Friendly Navigation:

- Ensure that your navigation is optimized for mobile devices. Mobile-friendly navigation might involve a hamburger menu or condensed menu options to accommodate smaller screens without sacrificing user experience.

11. **Consistent Design Elements:**

- Maintain consistency in design elements across pages. This includes consistent placement of the navigation menu, uniform fonts, and cohesive color schemes. Consistency fosters familiarity and helps users feel comfortable as they navigate your site.

12. **User Testing:**

- Conduct user testing or gather feedback from individuals unfamiliar with your website. This process can highlight potential navigation challenges and provide insights into how users perceive and interact with your content structure.

By following these steps, you can create a well-organized and user-friendly structure for your website's content. A thoughtfully structured website enhances user satisfaction, encourages exploration, and contributes to the overall success of your online platform.

- **Customize Design: Choosing templates, colors, and fonts.**

Customizing the design of your website is a key step in establishing its visual identity and enhancing user engagement. By choosing the right templates, colors, and fonts, you can create a cohesive and appealing aesthetic that aligns with your brand or personal style. Here's a guide to help you customize the design of your website:

1. **Choose a Template:**

• Begin by selecting a template that suits the purpose and vibe of your website. Templates provide a pre-designed framework that you can customize. Google Sites offers various templates, including those for portfolios, business sites, and personal pages.

2. **Consider Your Brand or Theme:**

• If your website represents a brand or has a specific theme, choose a template that aligns with these elements. Consider factors such as color schemes, layouts, and overall aesthetics that complement your brand identity or theme.

3. **Explore Template Options:**

• Google Sites offers a range of template options. Take the time to explore different templates and preview how they look with your content. Consider factors like the placement of navigation menus, header styles, and the overall structure.

4. **Customize Colors:**

• Tailor the color scheme of your website to match your brand or personal preferences. Google Sites allows you to customize colors for various elements, including backgrounds, text, and links. Consistent and harmonious color choices contribute to a polished look.

5. **Choose Fonts Wisely:**

- Select fonts that enhance readability and complement the overall design. Google Sites provides a variety of font options. Consider using a combination of fonts for headings and body text, ensuring a visually appealing and cohesive presentation.

6. **Maintain Consistency:**

- Maintain consistency in design elements across your website. Use the same color palette and fonts throughout to create a unified and professional appearance. Consistency contributes to brand recognition and a positive user experience.

7. **Header and Footer Customization:**

- Customize the header and footer sections of your website. Add a logo or banner to the header, and include essential information or links in the footer. These areas provide valuable real estate for branding and navigation.

8. **Background Images or Colors:**

- Consider using background images or colors to enhance the visual appeal of your website. Background elements can be applied to the entire page or specific sections. Ensure that backgrounds complement the overall design without overpowering the content.

9. **Experiment with Layouts:**

- Google Sites allows for flexible layout options. Experiment with different layouts to find the one that best showcases your content. Grids, columns, and sections can be adjusted to create a visually dynamic and organized presentation.

10. **Preview and Test:**

- Before finalizing your design, use the preview function to see how your website will appear to visitors. Test the design on various devices to ensure responsiveness and adjust any elements that may need refinement.

11. **Optimize for Mobile Viewing:**

- Given the prevalence of mobile devices, ensure that your design is optimized for smaller screens. Google Sites automatically adjusts layouts for mobile viewing, but it's essential to review and make adjustments as needed.

12. **Seek Feedback:**

- Once you've customized your design, seek feedback from others. Ask for opinions on the visual appeal, readability, and overall user experience. Constructive feedback can help you make final refinements before launching your website.

By carefully choosing templates, colors, and fonts, you can create a visually captivating and cohesive design for your website. The customized design contributes to a positive first impression, reinforces your brand identity, and encourages visitors to engage with your content.

- **Mobile-Friendly Design: Ensuring accessibility for all users.**

In today's digital landscape, optimizing your website for mobile devices is imperative to reach a broad audience and provide a positive user experience. A mobile-friendly design ensures that visitors can access and navigate your site seamlessly on smartphones and tablets. Here's a guide to help you ensure accessibility for all users through mobile-friendly design:

1. **Responsive Design:**

- Implement a responsive design approach, allowing your website to adapt to various screen sizes and resolutions. This ensures that content remains visually appealing and functional, whether viewed on a desktop, tablet, or smartphone.

2. **Mobile Preview:**

- Use the mobile preview feature provided by Google Sites to assess how your website appears on smaller screens. This allows you to identify and address any potential issues related to layout, spacing, and content visibility.

3. **Simplified Navigation:**

•   Streamline your navigation menu for mobile users. Consider using a hamburger menu (three horizontal lines) to condense navigation options. This approach maximizes screen space and provides a clean, user-friendly interface.

4. **Optimize Images and Media:**

•   Optimize images and media files for faster loading on mobile devices. Compress images without compromising quality, and consider using smaller file formats. This enhances page loading speed, a crucial factor for mobile users.

5. **Readable Font Sizes:**

•   Ensure that text is easily readable on smaller screens by using appropriate font sizes. Aim for a font size that is comfortable for reading without zooming. Google Sites automatically adjusts font sizes for mobile viewing, but verify and adjust as needed.

6. **Touch-Friendly Buttons:**

•   Design buttons and interactive elements to be touch-friendly. Ensure sufficient spacing between clickable elements to prevent accidental clicks. Touch-friendly design enhances the overall user experience for mobile visitors.

7. **Prioritize Content:**

- Prioritize essential content for mobile users. Display key information prominently and consider condensing or reorganizing content to fit smaller screens. This ensures that mobile visitors quickly access the most relevant information.

8. **Vertical Scrolling:**

- Embrace vertical scrolling as the primary navigation method for mobile users. Avoid horizontal scrolling, as it can be inconvenient and less intuitive on small screens. Vertical scrolling is a natural and expected behavior for mobile devices.

9. **Test Cross-Browser Compatibility:**

- Test your website's compatibility across various browsers and devices. Different browsers may interpret responsive design elements differently, so thorough testing ensures a consistent experience for all users.

10. **Minimize Pop-Ups:**

- Minimize the use of pop-ups or interstitials that may disrupt the mobile user experience. If necessary, ensure that pop-ups are easy to close and do not interfere with navigation or content access.

11. **Optimize Forms for Mobile Input:**

• If your website includes forms, optimize them for mobile input. Use input fields that are easy to select, and consider implementing features like autofill to simplify the form-filling process for mobile users.

12. **Regular Testing:**

• Conduct regular testing on actual mobile devices to simulate the experience of your mobile audience. This hands-on approach allows you to identify and address any issues that may arise specifically on mobile platforms.

By implementing these strategies, you can create a mobile-friendly design that ensures accessibility for all users. Prioritizing the mobile user experience contributes to higher user satisfaction, improved search engine rankings, and a broader reach for your website.

• **Template Selection: Choosing the right template for your needs.**

Selecting the right template is a pivotal decision in the website creation process. The template serves as the foundation for your site, influencing its visual appeal and overall structure. Here's a guide to help you choose the right template for your specific needs on Google Sites:

1. **Understand Your Website's Purpose:**

- Clearly define the purpose and goals of your website before selecting a template. Whether it's a portfolio, business site, personal blog, or project showcase, understanding your website's purpose guides your template choice.

2. **Explore Available Templates:**

- Google Sites offers a variety of templates designed for different purposes. Explore the available templates by navigating to the "Template gallery" during the site creation process. Preview templates to get a sense of their layout and design.

3. **Consider Visual Appeal:**

- Assess the visual appeal of each template and consider how it aligns with your aesthetic preferences or brand identity. Look for templates with color schemes, fonts, and layouts that resonate with the tone you want to convey.

4. **Evaluate Layout Options:**

- Examine the layout options provided by each template. Consider the placement of headers, navigation menus, and content sections. Choose a layout that complements your content and enhances its presentation.

5. **Mobile Responsiveness:**

• Ensure that the template is mobile-responsive. Mobile responsiveness is crucial for reaching users on various devices, and Google Sites automatically adjusts templates for mobile viewing. Verify the responsiveness to guarantee a seamless experience.

6. **Template Customization:**

• Consider the level of customization allowed by each template. While all templates can be customized to some extent, some may offer more flexibility in terms of color customization, font choices, and layout adjustments.

7. **Content Organization:**

• Analyze how each template organizes content. Some templates may prioritize a single-page design, while others provide multiple pages or a hierarchical structure. Choose a template that aligns with your preferred content organization.

8. **Multimedia Integration:**

• If your website includes a significant amount of multimedia content, such as images or videos, assess how well the template integrates and displays these elements. Ensure that the template enhances the presentation of your multimedia content.

9.   **Think About Navigation:**

•	Consider the navigation features provided by each template. Efficient and user-friendly navigation is crucial for a positive user experience. Templates may offer horizontal or vertical navigation menus, and some may utilize a hamburger menu for mobile users.

10. **Check Template Reviews:**

•	If available, check reviews or feedback from other users who have used the template. Their experiences can provide insights into any potential limitations or advantages of a particular template.

11. **Scalability:**

•	Think about the scalability of the template. Choose a template that can grow with your content. Consider how well the template accommodates additional pages and new sections without sacrificing visual coherence.

12. **Align with Branding:**

•	If your website represents a brand, ensure that the template aligns with your branding elements. Consistent use of brand colors, logos, and fonts reinforces your brand identity across the site.

By considering these factors, you can make an informed decision when selecting a template for your Google Sites website. The right template sets the stage for an engaging and visually appealing online presence that aligns with your specific goals and audience preferences.

CHAPTER 3

GETTING STARTED WITH BUILDING YOUR SITE

- **Create Your First Page: Step-by-step guide to page creation.**

Creating your first page on Google Sites is an exciting step towards building your website. Follow this step-by-step guide to successfully create your inaugural page:

1. **Sign In to Google Sites:**

- Open your web browser and navigate to Google Sites (sites.google.com). Sign in with your Google account credentials.

2. **Access Your Google Sites Dashboard:**

- Once signed in, you'll be directed to the Google Sites dashboard. Click on the "+" icon or the "Create" button to initiate the page creation process.

3. **Choose a Blank Page or Template:**

- Google Sites provides the option to start with a blank page or use a template. Choose "Blank" if you want to create a page from scratch or select a template that aligns with the purpose of your page.

4. **Name Your Page:**

- Give your page a descriptive and relevant name. The page name is usually displayed in the navigation menu and browser tabs, so choose a name that clearly communicates the content or purpose of the page.

5. **Add Content Blocks:**

- Once your page is created, you'll be in the editing mode. Start by adding content blocks. Click on the "+" icon to reveal a menu of content options, including text, images, and other elements. Choose the content block you want to add to your page.

6. **Edit Text and Add Headings:**

- Click on the text box to edit and add your own text. Format the text using the toolbar options that appear, including bold, italic, and underline. Use headings to structure your content by selecting the appropriate heading style.

7. **Insert Images and Media:**

- To add images or media, click on the "+" icon, choose "Image," and upload your image. You can also embed videos, Google Drive files, or other multimedia elements to enhance your page.

8. **Create Hyperlinks:**

- If you want to link to other pages or external websites, highlight the text you want to turn into a hyperlink, click on the link icon, and enter the URL. This allows users to navigate seamlessly between pages or external resources.

9. **Format and Customize:**

- Use the formatting options to customize the appearance of your text, including font size, color, and alignment. Experiment with the customization features to make your content visually appealing.

10. **Organize with Sections:**

- If your page has multiple sections, use the "Sections" feature to organize and separate content. Click on the "+" icon, choose "Section," and add a new section to your page.

11. **Save Your Work:**

- Periodically save your work by clicking the "Save" button. This ensures that your progress is preserved, and you can continue editing without fear of losing changes.

12. **Preview Your Page:**

- Before publishing, use the preview feature to see how your page will appear to visitors. This allows you to catch any formatting issues and make adjustments as needed.

13. **Publish Your Page:**

- Once you're satisfied with your page, click on the "Publish" button to make it live. Confirm the visibility settings, and your page will be accessible to others.

14. **Share Your Page:**

- Share your newly created page by clicking on the "Share" button. Enter the email addresses of individuals you want to collaborate with or share the link directly. Adjust permissions to control who can view or edit the page.

Congratulations! You've successfully created your first page on Google Sites. As you become more familiar with the platform, explore additional features such as page settings, access permissions, and the overall site structure to further enhance your website.

- **Customize Page Settings: Layout, permissions, and more.**

Fine-tuning page settings in Google Sites allows you to tailor the layout, control permissions, and optimize the overall user experience. Here's a step-by-step guide to customize your page settings:

1. **Access the Page Settings:**

• While in edit mode, locate the settings icon (gear symbol) in the upper right corner of the page. Click on it to access the page settings menu.

2. **Page Information:**

• Update the page information, including the page name and any description. This information is helpful for both users and search engines, providing context about the page's content.

3. **Change the Page URL:**

• If you want to customize the URL of your page, click on "Change" next to the URL field. Choose a concise and descriptive URL that reflects the content or purpose of the page.

4. **Select a Layout:**

• Under the "Layout" section, choose the desired page layout. Google Sites offers various layout options, allowing you to present content in a way that suits your preferences. Experiment with different layouts to find the most suitable one.

5. **Adjust Background and Themes:**

• Customize the background color or image of your page. Click on "Themes, Colors, and Fonts" to access options for adjusting the overall appearance of your page. Experiment with different themes to find the one that complements your content.

6. **Set Permissions:**

- Determine who can view and edit your page by adjusting the permissions. Click on "Access," and a menu will appear where you can specify permissions. Choose from options like "Anyone with the link can view" or limit access to specific individuals.

7. **Page Visibility:**

- Decide whether your page should be visible on the navigation menu. Toggle the "Show in navigation" switch to control whether the page is displayed in the site's navigation menu.

8. **Custom Header Type:**

- If your page has a header, select the header type that best suits your content. Options may include titles, banners, or none, depending on your design preferences.

9. **Enable or Disable Comments:**

- Determine whether you want viewers to leave comments on your page. Toggle the "Allow comments" switch based on your preferences. This feature is particularly useful for fostering interaction and feedback.

10. **Page Sections:**

- Manage the page sections by clicking on "Sections." This allows you to organize and reorder sections within your page, contributing to a well-structured layout.

11. **Page Footer:**

- Customize the page footer by clicking on "Footer." Add information such as copyright details, contact information, or links to other pages.

12. **Save Changes:**

- After making adjustments, don't forget to save your changes. Click on the "Save" button to ensure that your customized page settings are preserved.

13. **Preview Your Page:**

- Before publishing, use the preview feature to see how your page will appear with the updated settings. This helps you identify any potential issues and make additional adjustments if necessary.

14. **Publish Your Changes:**

- Once you're satisfied with the customized settings, click on "Publish" to make the changes live. Confirm the visibility settings and permissions before publishing.

By customizing your page settings, you can create a visually appealing and user-friendly experience for visitors. Whether adjusting layout preferences, controlling access, or refining the overall appearance, these settings contribute to the effectiveness and professionalism of your Google Sites page.

- **Add Gadgets and Features: Incorporating useful elements.**

Enhance the functionality and interactivity of your Google Sites page by incorporating gadgets and features. These elements can range from interactive forms to dynamic content displays. Here's a step-by-step guide to adding gadgets and features to your page:

1. **Access Edit Mode:**

- Ensure you are in edit mode on your Google Sites page. Click the "Edit" button to enter the editing interface.

2. **Click on the "+" Icon:**

- In the location where you want to add a gadget or feature, click on the "+" icon to open the insert menu.

3. **Choose "Embed":**

- Select "Embed" from the menu. This option allows you to embed various types of content, including gadgets and interactive elements.

4. **Insert a URL or Embed Code:**

- Depending on the gadget or feature you want to add, you may need to provide a URL or embed code. For example, if you're adding a YouTube video, paste the video URL. If you're incorporating a custom gadget, paste the provided embed code.

5. **Adjust Size and Position:**

- After pasting the URL or embed code, you can adjust the size and position of the embedded element. Use the handles to resize, and drag the element to reposition it on the page.

6. **Preview Your Changes:**

- Before saving, use the preview feature to see how the embedded gadget or feature will appear to visitors. This allows you to make any necessary adjustments to size or positioning.

7. **Add Google Workspace Elements:**

- Utilize Google Workspace elements such as Google Drive files, Google Calendar, or Google Sheets. Click on the "+" icon, select "Google Workspace," and choose the desired element to embed. Configure settings and insert the element onto your page.

8. **Insert a Google Form:**

- If you want to gather information through a form, click on the "+" icon, choose "Forms," and select "Google Forms."

This allows you to embed a Google Form directly into your page. Adjust form settings as needed.

9.   **Include an Image Carousel:**

•   Enhance visual appeal by adding an image carousel. Click on the "+" icon, choose "Image," and select "Image Carousel." Upload multiple images, and configure settings such as transition effects and speed.

10. **Integrate Google Maps:**

•   If your page involves location information, add a Google Map. Click on the "+" icon, choose "Maps," and select "Google Maps." Enter the location details, customize the map's appearance, and insert it onto your page.

11. **Embed Calendars:**

•   Showcase events or schedules by embedding a Google Calendar. Click on the "+" icon, choose "Calendar," and select "Google Calendar." Configure calendar settings and insert it into your page.

12. **Add a Table of Contents:**

•   Improve navigation within lengthy pages by adding a table of contents. Click on the "+" icon, choose "Table of Contents," and insert it onto your page. This feature automatically generates links to different sections.

13. **Insert a Divider:**

- Use dividers to visually separate content sections. Click on the "+" icon, choose "Divider," and insert it into the desired location on your page.

14. **Save Your Changes:**

- Once you've added and configured the desired gadgets and features, save your changes by clicking the "Save" button.

15. **Publish Your Page:**

- After saving, publish your page to make the changes live. Confirm the visibility settings and permissions to ensure the embedded gadgets and features are accessible to your audience.

By incorporating these gadgets and features, you can make your Google Sites page more dynamic, engaging, and functional. Experiment with different elements to create a customized and interactive user experience.

- **Real-Time Editing: Collaborate seamlessly with team members.**

Google Sites facilitates real-time editing, enabling effortless collaboration among team members. Here's a guide on how to leverage this feature for seamless teamwork:

1. **Access Your Google Sites Dashboard:**

•   Sign in to your Google account and navigate to Google Sites (sites.google.com). Open the website you want to collaborate on.

2. **Click on "Edit" or the Pencil Icon:**

•   Locate the "Edit" button or the pencil icon on the top right corner of the page. Click on it to enter edit mode.

3. **Invite Collaborators:**

•   Click on the "Share" button to invite team members to collaborate. Enter the email addresses of individuals you want to collaborate with. Specify their access level—whether they can edit or view only.

4. **Adjust Permissions:**

•   Choose whether collaborators can edit the site or only view it. Adjust permissions accordingly to control the level of access team members have.

5. **Collaborate in Real Time:**

•   Once collaborators are added, you can simultaneously edit the site in real time. Changes made by one team member are instantly visible to others. Collaborators can contribute text, add images, and make modifications concurrently.

6. **Use Comments for Communication:**

- Encourage communication by utilizing the commenting feature. Highlight a section of text or an element, click on the comment icon, and leave remarks. Collaborators can respond to comments and engage in discussions.

7. **Track Changes with Revision History:**

- Monitor changes made by team members using the "File" menu and selecting "See revision history." This feature allows you to review edits, revert to previous versions, and track the evolution of the site.

8. **Insert Action Items or To-Do Lists:**

- Collaborate more effectively by incorporating action items or to-do lists directly into the site. Use text boxes, lists, or gadgets to create a dynamic task list that team members can update in real time.

9. **Coordinate Section Ownership:**

- Divide the website into sections and assign ownership to different team members. This way, each member can be responsible for specific content or pages, streamlining the collaborative process.

10. **Provide Context with Page Comments:**

• Add context to specific pages by using the "Page comments" feature. Team members can leave comments on specific pages, providing additional information or feedback related to that page's content.

11. **Collaborate on Embedded Google Workspace Elements:**

• If your site includes embedded Google Workspace elements like Google Docs, Sheets, or Slides, collaborators can edit these elements in real time directly within the site.

12. **Review and Accept Changes:**

• If there are conflicting edits, collaborators can review changes and accept or reject them. This ensures that the final version reflects the agreed-upon content.

13. **Save Changes and Publish:**

• Once collaboration is complete, save changes and publish the site to make the updated content live. Confirm visibility settings and permissions before publishing.

14. **Regularly Communicate and Update:**

• Foster a collaborative environment by regularly communicating with team members. Update each other on progress, share ideas, and address any questions or concerns that arise during the editing process.

By embracing real-time editing on Google Sites, your team can work cohesively, fostering creativity, and efficiently producing a well-crafted website. This collaborative approach enhances communication, accelerates project timelines, and ensures that everyone's input contributes to the success of the site.

- **Multimedia Insertion: Adding images, videos, and more.**

Enhance the visual appeal and engagement of your Google Sites page by incorporating multimedia elements. Here's a step-by-step guide on how to add images, videos, and other multimedia to your site:

1. **Access Edit Mode:**

- Open your Google Sites page and click on the "Edit" button or the pencil icon to enter edit mode.

2. **Insert an Image:**

- Click on the "+" icon where you want to insert an image. Choose "Image" from the menu. Upload an image from your computer or select one from your Google Drive. Adjust the size and position as needed.

3. **Add Image Captions:**

- Enhance your images with captions. Click on the inserted image, then click on the "Insert" menu and choose "Text box." Type your caption and position it near the image.

4. **Embed a Video:**

- To embed a video, click on the "+" icon, choose "Embed," and paste the video URL or embed code. You can embed videos from YouTube, Google Drive, or other supported platforms.

5. **Insert a Slideshow:**

- Create dynamic visual presentations by adding a slideshow. Click on the "+" icon, choose "Slides," and select "Google Slides." Choose the presentation you want to embed, and customize settings such as autoplay and size.

6. **Incorporate Google Maps:**

- Embed a Google Map to provide location information. Click on the "+" icon, choose "Maps," and select "Google Maps." Enter the location details, customize the appearance, and insert the map.

7. **Include Google Calendar:**

- Showcase events or schedules by embedding a Google Calendar. Click on the "+" icon, choose "Calendar," and select "Google Calendar." Configure calendar settings and insert it into your page.

8. **Upload PDFs and Documents:**

- If you want to share documents or PDFs, click on the "+" icon, choose "Embed," and select "Google Drive." Upload your document to Google Drive, copy the link, and paste it to embed the document.

9. **Add Image Carousels:**

- Create visually engaging image carousels. Click on the "+" icon, choose "Image," and select "Image Carousel." Upload multiple images, and customize settings such as transition effects and speed.

10. **Integrate Forms:**

- If you need to gather information, click on the "+" icon, choose "Forms," and select "Google Forms." Embed a Google Form directly into your page, and adjust form settings as needed.

11. **Embed Social Media Feeds:**

- Showcase your social media activity by embedding feeds. Click on the "+" icon, choose "Embed," and paste the embed code from your social media platform (e.g., Twitter, Instagram). Adjust the size and position.

12. **Insert Audio Files:**

- Enhance your page with audio elements. Click on the "+" icon, choose "Audio," and upload an audio file. Customize settings such as autoplay and loop to create a seamless audio experience.

13. **Use Custom HTML:**

- For advanced users, click on the "+" icon, choose "Embed," and select "Embed code." Insert custom HTML code to integrate third-party widgets, plugins, or elements not directly supported by Google Sites.

14. **Preview Your Changes:**

- Before saving, use the preview feature to see how the multimedia elements will appear to visitors. This allows you to make any necessary adjustments to size or positioning.

15. **Save Changes and Publish:**

- Once you've added and configured the multimedia elements, save your changes by clicking the "Save" button. Publish your page to make the multimedia elements live. Confirm the visibility settings and permissions.

By incorporating these multimedia elements, you can create a visually rich and interactive Google Sites page that captures the attention of your audience. Experiment with different elements to find the combination that best complements your content and engages your visitors.

CHAPTER 4

COLLABORATING ON GOOGLE SITES

- **Collaborative Features: Enhancing teamwork on projects.**

Google Sites offers a range of collaborative features that facilitate seamless teamwork on projects. Here's a comprehensive guide on leveraging these features to enhance collaboration:

1. **Shared Access and Editing:**

- Share your Google Sites project with team members by clicking on the "Share" button. Enter their email addresses and assign access levels. Collaborators can simultaneously edit the site in real time, fostering a collaborative environment.

2. **Comments and Feedback:**

- Encourage communication by using the commenting feature. Highlight a section of text or an element, click on the comment icon, and leave remarks. Team members can respond to comments, ask questions, and provide feedback directly within the page.

3. **Task Assignments with Action Items:**

- Integrate task assignments directly into your site by using text boxes, lists, or gadgets. Create action items or to-do lists that team members can update in real time. This ensures everyone is aware of their responsibilities.

4. Ownership and Section Assignment:

- Divide your Google Sites project into sections and assign ownership to different team members. This helps distribute responsibilities and allows individuals to focus on specific content or pages.

5. Revision History:

- Track changes made by team members using the "File" menu and selecting "See revision history." This feature allows you to review edits, revert to previous versions, and monitor the evolution of the project.

6. Embed Google Workspace Elements:

- Collaborate seamlessly on embedded Google Workspace elements like Google Docs, Sheets, or Slides. Team members can edit these elements in real time directly within the Google Sites project.

7. Coordinated Editing in Google Docs:

- Integrate Google Docs into your project for collaborative writing and editing. Click on the "+" icon, select "Google Docs," and embed a document. Team members can contribute to the document simultaneously.

8. **Live Chat with Google Meet:**

- Enhance real-time collaboration by incorporating Google Meet directly into your site. Click on the "+" icon, select "Embed," and paste the Google Meet link. This allows team members to join video meetings without leaving the project.

9. **Page-Level Comments:**

- Provide context to specific pages by using the "Page comments" feature. Team members can leave comments on specific pages, offering additional information or feedback related to that page's content.

10. **Integrated Google Calendar:**

- Embed a shared Google Calendar to keep the team informed about deadlines, events, and project milestones. Click on the "+" icon, choose "Calendar," and select "Google Calendar." Configure calendar settings and insert it into the project.

11. **Shared Drive Integration:**

- Leverage Google Drive integration by embedding folders or files directly into your project. Click on the "+" icon, select "Embed," and choose "Google Drive." Select the files or folders you want to share with the team.

12. **Collaborative Forms and Surveys:**

• Embed Google Forms to collect input from team members. Click on the "+" icon, choose "Forms," and select "Google Forms." Embed the form directly into the project, and team members can fill it out without leaving the site.

13. **Shared Resources Section:**

• Create a dedicated section for shared resources such as documents, templates, or guidelines. Use text boxes, links, or embedded Google Drive elements to centralize important information for the team.

14. **Team Communication with Chat:**

• Foster real-time communication by adding a chat feature to your project. Click on the "+" icon, select "Chat," and insert a chat box. Team members can use this feature for quick communication and coordination.

15. **Regular Updates and Team Discussions:**

• Encourage regular team updates and discussions within the Google Sites project. Create dedicated pages or sections for team discussions, progress updates, and collaborative brainstorming.

By utilizing these collaborative features, your team can efficiently work together on projects, streamline communication, and benefit from a centralized platform for information sharing. Google Sites becomes a dynamic hub where team members can contribute, communicate, and collaborate effectively.

- **Team Access Management: Set permissions and invite collaborators.**

Efficient team access management is crucial for maintaining control and security over your Google Sites project. Here's a step-by-step guide on how to set permissions and invite collaborators:

1. **Access Your Google Sites Project:**

- Sign in to your Google account and navigate to Google Sites. Open the project for which you want to manage team access.

2. **Click on "Share":**

- In the top-right corner of your project, click on the "Share" button. This will open the sharing settings menu.

3. **Enter Collaborators' Email Addresses:**

- In the sharing settings menu, enter the email addresses of the individuals you want to invite as collaborators. Google will suggest contacts as you type.

4. **Set Access Levels:**

- For each collaborator, choose the appropriate access level. Google Sites offers two main access levels:

- **Editor:** Can edit the site, add and remove content, and collaborate in real time.

- **Viewer:** Can only view the site but cannot make edits.

5. **Adjust Advanced Settings:**

- Click on "Advanced" to access additional settings. Here, you can:

- **Prevent Editors from Changing Access and Adding New People:** Ensures that only the owner can manage access.

- **Disable Options to Download, Print, and Copy for Commenters and Viewers:** Adds an extra layer of control over document access.

6. **Notify Collaborators:**

- Check the box to notify collaborators via email. This sends an email to each collaborator with a link to access the project. You can also include a custom message in the email.

7. **Copy Link to Share:**

- If you prefer, you can copy a shareable link and send it manually to collaborators. Be cautious with this method, as anyone with the link can access the project based on the permissions you set.

8. **Share with Google Groups:**

- For convenience, you can share your project with a Google Group. Simply enter the email address of the Google Group, and all members of the group will gain access based on the specified permissions.

9. **Review and Confirm Settings:**

- Before finalizing, review the list of collaborators and their assigned access levels. Ensure that the settings align with your intentions for the project.

10. **Click "Send":**

- Once you've adjusted the settings and added collaborators, click on the "Send" button to invite them. Collaborators will receive an email notification and can access the project accordingly.

11. **Monitor Access and Changes:**

- Regularly monitor the list of collaborators and their access levels. If project requirements change, adjust access levels or remove collaborators as needed.

12. **Adjust Access for Specific Pages:**

- Google Sites allows you to set different access levels for specific pages. Click on the page you want to adjust, click on "Page settings," and adjust the access level as needed.

13. **Remove Collaborators:**

- If a collaborator's access is no longer required, you can remove them from the project. In the sharing settings menu, locate the collaborator and click on the "X" next to their name.

14. **Access History and Permissions Audit:**

- Track access history and permissions changes by clicking on "Access" and selecting "Viewer history" or "Editor history." This provides an audit trail of who accessed the project and when.

15. **Regularly Review and Update:**

- Collaborators and project requirements may change over time. Regularly review and update access settings to ensure that only authorized individuals have the necessary permissions.

By following these steps, you can effectively manage team access to your Google Sites project, promoting collaboration while maintaining control and security. Efficient access management ensures that your project remains organized, secure, and accessible to the right individuals.

- **Google Workspace Integration: Streamlining collaboration.**

Integrating Google Workspace into your Google Sites project enhances collaboration and productivity. Follow these steps to seamlessly integrate Google Workspace elements into your site:

1. **Embed Google Docs:**

- Click on the "+" icon, select "Google Docs," and choose the document you want to embed. Team members can collaboratively edit the document directly within the Google Sites project.

2. **Incorporate Google Sheets:**

- Add Google Sheets to your project by clicking on the "+" icon, selecting "Google Sheets," and choosing the desired spreadsheet. This integration allows real-time collaboration on data and calculations.

3. **Embed Google Slides:**

- Enhance presentations by embedding Google Slides. Click on the "+" icon, select "Google Slides," and choose the presentation to embed. Team members can collaboratively work on the slides within the project.

4. **Include Google Forms:**

- Embed Google Forms directly into your site for streamlined data collection. Click on the "+" icon, select "Forms," and choose the Google Form you want to incorporate. Responses will be collected in the associated Google Sheets.

5. **Integrate Google Calendar:**

- Showcase events, deadlines, and schedules by embedding a Google Calendar. Click on the "+" icon, select "Calendar," and choose the Google Calendar to embed. Team members can view and interact with the calendar within the project.

6. **Embed Google Maps:**

- Enhance location-based information by embedding Google Maps. Click on the "+" icon, select "Maps," and choose the Google Map to embed. This integration provides a dynamic way to showcase geographical data.

7. **Collaborate with Google Drive:**

- Integrate Google Drive by clicking on the "+" icon, selecting "Embed," and choosing "Google Drive." Embed folders or files directly into your project, providing easy access to shared resources.

8. **Utilize Google Hangouts or Google Meet:**

• Foster real-time communication by incorporating Google Hangouts or Google Meet directly into your project. Click on the "+" icon, select "Embed," and paste the link for Hangouts or Meet.

9. **Embed Google Drawings:**

• Add visual elements by embedding Google Drawings. Click on the "+" icon, select "Google Drawings," and choose the drawing to embed. This feature is useful for diagrams, flowcharts, or custom illustrations.

10. **Collaborative Editing with Google Workspace:**

• Leverage real-time collaboration by using Google Workspace elements directly within your Google Sites project. Team members can edit documents, spreadsheets, presentations, and more simultaneously.

11. **Customize Permissions for Workspace Elements:**

• Adjust permissions for embedded Google Workspace elements based on your collaboration needs. Click on the element, choose "Access," and modify settings to control who can view or edit the integrated content.

12. **Link to Shared Google Workspace Elements:**

• If embedding is not necessary, you can link to shared Google Workspace elements. Create hyperlinks within your pages that direct team members to the respective documents, sheets, or slides.

13. **Collaborate on Task Lists with Google Keep:**

• Embed Google Keep notes with task lists directly into your project. Click on the "+" icon, select "Google Keep," and choose the note to embed. Team members can update and collaborate on tasks.

14. **Access Forms and Sheets for Surveys:**

• If your project involves surveys or data collection, embed Google Forms for data input and Google Sheets for data analysis. Click on the "+" icon, select "Forms" or "Sheets," and choose the respective elements.

15. **Regularly Update and Sync:**

• Ensure that embedded Google Workspace elements are regularly updated and synced with the latest changes. This ensures that your team has access to the most current information within the project.

By integrating Google Workspace seamlessly into your Google Sites project, you create a centralized hub for collaboration, enabling team members to work efficiently, share resources, and contribute to the project's success.

- **Version Control: Understand version history and recovery.**

Effectively managing version control in your Google Sites project is essential for tracking changes, reverting to previous states, and ensuring the integrity of your content. Follow these steps to navigate version history and recovery:

1. **Access Version History:**

- While in edit mode on your Google Sites project, click on the "File" menu, and select "See revision history." This opens the version history panel on the right side of the screen.

2. **Review Version Timeline:**

- The version history panel displays a timeline of changes made to your project. Each revision is marked with a timestamp and the collaborator's name who made the change. Scroll through the timeline to locate specific versions.

3. **Explore Detailed Changes:**

- Click on a specific timestamp to explore detailed changes made in that version. The panel highlights additions, deletions, and modifications, providing a comprehensive overview of content edits.

4. **Revert to a Previous Version:**

• To revert to a previous version, select the timestamp of the desired version, and click on "Restore this version." This action replaces the current version with the selected one. Confirm the restoration when prompted.

5. **Review Editors and Changes:**

• The version history panel also displays a list of editors who contributed to each version. Click on an editor's name to see the changes they made. This feature helps track individual contributions to the project.

6. **Name Versions for Clarity:**

• To make version identification easier, consider naming significant versions. Click on the three dots next to a timestamp and select "Name this version." Enter a descriptive name for the version, such as "Project Milestone" or "Final Draft."

7. **Compare Versions:**

• Use the "Compare" button to compare two versions side by side. This feature highlights differences between versions, making it easier to identify specific changes and understand how the project has evolved.

8. **Create a Copy of a Version:**

- If you want to preserve a specific version without reverting to it, click on the three dots next to a timestamp and select "Make a copy." This creates a duplicate of the selected version, preserving it in the version history.

9. **Access Version History for Specific Pages:**

- If your project has multiple pages, you can access version history for specific pages. Click on the page name in the right panel, and then click on "See revision history" to review and restore versions for that specific page.

10. **Regularly Save and Describe Changes:**

- To maintain a clear version history, regularly save your project, especially after making significant changes. When prompted to describe changes, provide clear and concise descriptions to aid in version identification.

11. **Collaborate Responsibly:**

- Encourage collaborators to follow responsible editing practices. Remind them to save changes, name versions when necessary, and provide meaningful descriptions of their edits. This fosters a collaborative environment with a well-documented version history.

12. Monitor Project Evolution:

• Regularly review the version history to monitor the evolution of your project. This helps you understand how content has changed over time and allows for strategic decision-making regarding project direction.

13. Use Version Control for Collaborative Projects:

• For larger projects with multiple collaborators, version control becomes even more crucial. Ensure that team members are familiar with version control practices and encourage them to utilize version history responsibly.

14. Educate Team Members:

• If you're working on a collaborative project, educate team members about version control features. Share information about accessing version history, reverting to previous versions, and preserving important milestones.

15. Regular Backups:

• While Google Sites automatically manages version history, consider regularly exporting and saving backups of your project as an extra precaution. This ensures that you have an external copy of your project at specific points in time.

By understanding and utilizing version control features in Google Sites, you can confidently manage changes, track project evolution, and ensure the integrity of your content throughout the collaborative editing process.

- **Best Practices for Collaboration: Ensure effective teamwork.**

Collaboration is the key to success in any project. Here are best practices to ensure effective teamwork on your Google Sites project:

1. **Establish Clear Goals:**

- Define clear project goals and objectives. Ensure that every team member understands the purpose of the project and how their contributions align with these goals.

2. **Use Collaborative Editing:**

- Leverage Google Sites' real-time editing feature to enable team members to collaborate seamlessly. Simultaneous editing allows for faster progress and encourages creativity.

3. **Communicate Effectively:**

- Foster open and transparent communication among team members. Use comments, chat features, and regular updates to keep everyone informed about progress, changes, and important decisions.

4. **Set Roles and Responsibilities:**

- Clearly define roles and responsibilities for each team member. Assign ownership of specific sections or tasks to individuals, streamlining accountability and minimizing confusion.

5. **Establish a Naming Convention:**

- Implement a naming convention for pages, files, and other project elements. Consistent naming makes it easier for team members to locate and identify specific items within the project.

6. **Educate Team Members:**

- Ensure that all team members are familiar with Google Sites and its features. Provide training or resources to help them navigate the platform effectively and utilize collaboration tools.

7. **Regularly Update and Save Changes:**

- Encourage team members to save changes regularly. When making significant updates, prompt them to describe changes, providing context in the version history for better understanding.

8. **Utilize Notifications:**

- Take advantage of notification features to keep team members informed about updates and changes. Notifications help prevent misunderstandings and keep everyone on the same page.

9. **Implement Version Control:**

• Teach team members how to use version control effectively. Make sure they understand how to access version history, revert changes if needed, and collaborate responsibly to maintain project integrity.

10. **Schedule Regular Check-Ins:**

• Organize regular check-ins or meetings to discuss progress, address concerns, and coordinate upcoming tasks. These meetings provide a platform for team members to share insights and updates.

11. **Encourage Collaboration on Google Workspace:**

• Promote the use of Google Workspace tools like Docs, Sheets, and Slides for collaborative content creation. Embed these elements directly into your Google Sites project for a seamless workflow.

12. **Establish a Centralized Resource Hub:**

• Create a dedicated page or section as a centralized hub for shared resources, guidelines, and important documents. This ensures that team members can easily access essential information.

13. Provide Constructive Feedback:

- Foster a positive and constructive feedback culture. Encourage team members to provide feedback on each other's work, focusing on improvement rather than criticism.

14. Celebrate Achievements:

- Acknowledge and celebrate achievements, milestones, and successful project outcomes. Recognizing team efforts boosts morale and motivation.

15. Document Decisions and Changes:

- Keep a record of important decisions, changes, and discussions. Documenting these details ensures that team members can reference historical information and understand the project's evolution.

16. Conduct Training Sessions:

- Conduct training sessions or workshops on Google Sites and collaboration best practices. Ensure that everyone on the team is equipped with the skills and knowledge needed for effective collaboration.

17. Resolve Conflicts Promptly:

- Address conflicts or disagreements promptly and constructively. Encourage open communication and provide a platform for team members to express concerns and find resolution.

18. **Regularly Review and Reflect:**

- Schedule periodic reviews to assess team dynamics, project progress, and collaboration effectiveness. Reflect on what is working well and identify areas for improvement.

By incorporating these best practices, you can create a collaborative environment that maximizes the potential of your team and ensures the success of your Google Sites project. Effective collaboration fosters creativity, accelerates project timelines, and contributes to a positive team culture.

CHAPTER 5

ENHANCING YOUR SITE WITH ADVANCED FEATURES

- **Advanced Layout Options: Customizing headers, footers, and more.**

Elevate the visual appeal and customization of your Google Sites project by exploring advanced layout options. Here's a guide on how to customize headers, footers, and other layout elements:

1. **Access Edit Mode:**

- Open your Google Sites project and click on the "Edit" button or the pencil icon to enter edit mode.

2. **Customize Header and Footer:**

- Click on the "Header" or "Footer" section to reveal customization options. Adjust background colors, insert images, or use custom text to personalize the header and footer of your site.

3. **Header and Footer Layout Options:**

- Experiment with different layout options for the header and footer. Choose between a single column, split, or full-width layout to find the design that best suits your project.

4. **Insert a Navigation Bar:**

- Enhance navigation by adding a custom navigation bar to your header. Click on the "+" icon, choose "Navigation," and select the type of navigation bar you want to include. Customize links and styles accordingly.

5. **Create Custom Navigation Links:**

- Add custom navigation links to your header or footer by using text boxes or links. This allows you to create a personalized navigation structure that aligns with your project's content.

6. **Adjust Section Layouts:**

- Customize the layout of individual sections within your pages. Click on the section, choose "Section layout," and select from options like one column, two columns, or full-width to control the structure of your content.

7. **Use Custom Spacers:**

- Fine-tune the spacing between elements by adding custom spacers. Click on the "+" icon, choose "Spacer," and adjust the dimensions to create precise spacing within your pages.

8. **Insert Columns:**

- Utilize columns for a more dynamic page layout. Click on the "+" icon, choose "Columns," and select the number of columns you want to include. Customize the width and distribution of columns as needed.

9. **Customize Backgrounds:**

• Give your project a unique look by customizing background colors or images. Click on the "Background" option in the "Theme" menu to access settings for modifying the overall background of your site.

10. **Experiment with Fonts and Colors:**

• Click on the "Theme" menu to explore font and color customization options. Experiment with different font styles, sizes, and color schemes to achieve a cohesive and visually appealing design.

11. **Embed Custom HTML/CSS:**

• For advanced users, click on the "+" icon, choose "Embed," and select "Embed code." This allows you to add custom HTML or CSS code to further customize the layout and appearance of your site.

12. **Add Custom Buttons:**

• Integrate custom buttons to create interactive elements on your pages. Click on the "+" icon, choose "Button," and customize the button's text, link, and appearance to suit your design.

13. **Customize Page Margins:**

• Adjust page margins to control the spacing between the content and the edges of your pages. Click on the "Page settings" option and navigate to the "Margins" section to modify these settings.

14. **Explore Advanced Header Options:**

- Click on the "Header" section and explore advanced options such as adding a site logo, adjusting transparency, or incorporating a background image. These options provide additional flexibility in customizing the header.

15. **Test Responsive Design:**

- Preview your site in different screen sizes to ensure a responsive design. Click on the preview icon and select different device options to see how your layout adapts to various screen resolutions.

16. **Save Changes and Publish:**

- Once you've customized the layout to your satisfaction, save your changes by clicking the "Save" button. Confirm the visibility settings and permissions before publishing your updated site.

By exploring these advanced layout options, you can create a visually stunning and customized Google Sites project that reflects your unique style and effectively communicates your content to your audience.

- **External Tools Integration: Adding widgets and third-party elements.**

Enhance the functionality of your Google Sites project by integrating external tools, widgets, and third-party elements. Here's a guide on how to seamlessly incorporate these elements:

1. **Identify External Tools:**

- Determine which external tools or widgets you want to integrate into your Google Sites project. Common examples include calendars, surveys, social media feeds, or custom HTML widgets.

2. **Click on the "+" Icon:**

- Enter edit mode on your Google Sites project and click on the "+" icon to open the insert menu.

3. **Choose "Embed":**

- Select the "Embed" option from the menu. This allows you to embed custom code or widgets into your pages.

4. **Paste Widget Code:**

- Obtain the embed code for the external tool or widget you want to add. Paste the code into the embed dialog box in Google Sites. Adjust dimensions and settings as needed.

5. **Preview and Adjust:**

•   Preview the embedded widget to ensure it displays correctly. Adjust the dimensions, alignment, or any other settings to seamlessly integrate the external tool into your page.

6. **Save Changes and Publish:**

•   Save your changes and publish your site to make the embedded external tool live. Confirm the visibility settings and permissions for the embedded element.

7. **Test Responsiveness:**

•   Test the responsiveness of the embedded widget by previewing your site on different devices. Ensure that the external tool adapts well to various screen sizes.

8. **Explore Google Sites Embeddable Elements:**

•   Google Sites supports embeddable elements from various Google services. Explore options like Google Calendar, Google Maps, Google Docs, and more. Click on the "+" icon, select "Embed," and choose the desired element.

9. **Utilize Google Workspace Integrations:**

•   Leverage Google Workspace integrations for seamless collaboration. Embed Google Docs, Sheets, Slides, or Forms directly into your project for real-time editing and collaboration.

10. **Customize External Tools Appearance:**

• If the external tool allows customization, explore options to match its appearance with the overall design of your Google Sites project. This creates a cohesive and integrated user experience.

Optimizing for Search Engines: Implementing SEO Best Practices

Boost the visibility of your Google Sites project with effective search engine optimization (SEO) practices. Follow these steps to optimize your site for search engines:

1. **Utilize Descriptive Page Titles:**

• Craft descriptive and concise page titles that accurately represent the content of each page. Include relevant keywords to enhance search engine visibility.

2. **Create SEO-Friendly URLs:**

• Customize page URLs to be SEO-friendly. Keep them short, use hyphens to separate words, and incorporate target keywords when possible.

3. **Add Meta Descriptions:**

• Write compelling meta descriptions for each page. These concise summaries provide users with information about the page's content and can improve click-through rates.

4. **Incorporate Heading Tags:**

• Use heading tags (H1, H2, H3, etc.) to structure your content. This not only improves readability but also helps search engines understand the hierarchy and importance of content.

5. **Optimize Image Alt Text:**

• Add descriptive alt text to images. This not only improves accessibility but also provides search engines with information about the content of the images.

6. **Include Internal Links:**

• Link to other relevant pages within your site using descriptive anchor text. Internal linking helps distribute authority across your site and enhances the user experience.

7. **Enable Google Analytics:**

• Integrate Google Analytics to track website traffic and user behavior. Analyzing data from Google Analytics helps you make informed decisions to improve your site's performance.

8. **Submit a Sitemap to Google Search Console:**

• Create and submit a sitemap of your Google Sites project to Google Search Console. This helps search engines index your pages more efficiently.

9. **Implement Responsive Design:**

• Ensure that your site is mobile-friendly and responsive. Google considers mobile compatibility as a ranking factor, and a responsive design improves the user experience across devices.

10. **Improve Page Loading Speed:**

• Optimize images, minimize code, and leverage browser caching to enhance your site's loading speed. Page speed is a crucial factor in both user experience and search engine rankings.

11. **Use HTTPS Encryption:**

• Enable HTTPS for your site to provide a secure browsing experience. Google gives preference to secure sites, and HTTPS is considered a ranking factor.

12. **Focus on Quality Content:**

• Produce high-quality, valuable, and relevant content. Search engines prioritize content that meets user intent, so focus on providing information that satisfies your audience's needs.

13. **Research and Use Relevant Keywords:**

• Conduct keyword research to identify terms relevant to your content. Incorporate these keywords naturally in your content, headings, and meta tags.

14. Regularly Update and Refresh Content:

- Keep your content up-to-date and relevant. Regularly update pages, add new content, and refresh existing information to maintain the relevance of your site.

15. Encourage Social Sharing:

- Integrate social media sharing buttons to encourage visitors to share your content. Social signals can indirectly influence search engine rankings.

16. Monitor and Adapt to Algorithm Changes:

- Stay informed about search engine algorithm updates and adapt your SEO strategy accordingly. Continuously monitor your site's performance and make adjustments as needed.

Interactive Elements: Engaging Visitors with Interactive Features

Capture and retain your audience's attention by incorporating interactive elements into your Google Sites project. Here's how to engage visitors with interactive features:

1. Add Image Carousels:

- Create visually appealing image carousels by clicking on the "+" icon, selecting "Image," and choosing "Image Carousel." Upload multiple images, and customize settings for a dynamic display.

2. **Embed Google Maps:**

- Enhance location-based information by embedding Google Maps. Click on the "+" icon, select "Maps," and choose "Google Maps." Enter location details, customize appearance, and insert the map.

3. **Integrate Google Calendar:**

- Showcase events and schedules by embedding a Google Calendar. Click on the "+" icon, choose "Calendar," and select "Google Calendar." Configure settings and insert it into your page.

4. **Embed YouTube Videos:**

- Enhance your content by embedding YouTube videos. Click on the "+" icon, select "Embed," and paste the YouTube video URL. Adjust settings for size and alignment.

5. **Incorporate Google Forms:**

- Engage visitors with interactive forms or surveys. Click on the "+" icon, select "Forms," and choose "Google Forms." Embed the form directly into your page for seamless interaction.

6. **Add Scrollable Text Boxes:**

- Create interactive text boxes with scrolling functionality. Click on the "+" icon, choose "Text box," and adjust settings to enable scrolling for longer text content.

7. Include Collapsible Sections:

- Enhance page organization by adding collapsible sections. Click on the "+" icon, choose "Collapsible text," and provide visitors with the option to expand or collapse specific content sections.

8. Embed Google Slides Presentations:

- Make your content more dynamic by embedding Google Slides presentations. Click on the "+" icon, select "Embed," and choose "Google Slides." Insert the presentation directly into your page.

9. Create Interactive Buttons:

- Utilize buttons to guide users to specific actions or sections. Click on the "+" icon, choose "Button," and customize the button's text, link, and appearance.

10. Implement Anchor Links:

- Create anchor links within your page to allow users to jump to specific sections. Click on the link icon, select "Link," and choose "Link to section." Pick the target section to create a smooth navigation experience.

11. Integrate Google Workspace Elements:

- Foster collaboration by embedding Google Workspace elements. Click on the "+" icon, select "Embed," and choose from Google Docs, Sheets, Slides, or Forms to seamlessly integrate collaborative features.

12. Include Interactive Images:

- Make images interactive by adding clickable hotspots. Click on the "+" icon, select "Image," and choose "Image Hotspot." Define areas in the image with links to provide additional information.

13. Utilize Google Drawings:

- Enhance visual communication by embedding Google Drawings. Click on the "+" icon, select "Google Drawings," and choose the drawing to embed. This is useful for creating custom illustrations or diagrams.

14. Embed Custom HTML/CSS for Interactivity:

- For advanced users, click on the "+" icon, choose "Embed," and select "Embed code." Incorporate custom HTML or CSS code to introduce interactive elements tailored to your specific needs.

15. Test Interactivity Across Devices:

- Ensure that interactive elements function seamlessly across different devices. Test your site's responsiveness and interactivity on various screen sizes to guarantee a positive user experience.

By incorporating these interactive elements, you create a dynamic and engaging user experience on your Google Sites project, encouraging visitors to explore and interact with your content.

Social Media Integration: Embedding Feeds for Increased Visibility

Boost your online presence by integrating social media feeds into your Google Sites project. Here's a guide on how to embed social media feeds for increased visibility:

1. **Select the Page:**

- Navigate to the page where you want to embed the social media feed in your Google Sites project.

2. **Click on the "+" Icon:**

- Enter edit mode and click on the "+" icon to open the insert menu.

3. **Choose "Embed":**

- Select the "Embed" option from the menu. This allows you to embed custom code, including social media feeds.

4. **Select Social Media Platform:**

- Choose the social media platform whose feed you want to embed (e.g., Twitter, Instagram, Facebook).

5. **Access Social Media Platform's Developer Tools:**

• Visit the developer tools section of the chosen social media platform to generate an embed code for the feed. Each platform has specific instructions for obtaining this code.

6. **Copy Embed Code:**

• Copy the provided embed code for the social media feed.

7. **Paste Code in Google Sites:**

• Paste the copied code into the embed dialog box in Google Sites. Adjust dimensions and settings as needed.

8. **Preview and Adjust:**

• Preview the embedded social media feed to ensure it displays correctly. Adjust the dimensions, alignment, or any other settings to seamlessly integrate the feed into your page.

9. **Save Changes and Publish:**

• Save your changes and publish your site to make the embedded social media feed live. Confirm the visibility settings and permissions for the embedded element.

10. **Test Responsiveness:**

- Test the responsiveness of the embedded social media feed by previewing your site on different devices. Ensure that the feed adapts well to various screen sizes.

11. **Customize Appearance:**

- Explore customization options provided by the social media platform to match the appearance of the embedded feed with the overall design of your Google Sites project.

12. **Consider Multiple Feeds:**

- Depending on your social media strategy, consider embedding feeds from multiple platforms to provide a comprehensive view of your online presence.

13. **Regularly Update Content:**

- Keep your social media content fresh and updated. Regularly post new content on your social media platforms to ensure that the embedded feeds on your site remain relevant.

14. **Encourage Interaction:**

- Encourage site visitors to interact with your social media content by including calls-to-action or prompts alongside the embedded feeds.

15. **Monitor Feed Performance:**

- Keep an eye on the performance of your embedded social media feeds. Check analytics on each platform to understand engagement and make adjustments as needed.

By integrating social media feeds into your Google Sites project, you enhance visibility, provide dynamic content, and create a cohesive online presence for your audience to explore.

CHAPTER 6

TROUBLESHOOTING AND FAQS

Navigate common issues and provide answers to frequently asked questions to ensure a smooth experience for users exploring your Google Sites project. Here's a guide on troubleshooting and FAQs:

1. **Troubleshooting Section:**

- Dedicate a section on your site to troubleshooting common issues. Include step-by-step guides or FAQs to assist users in resolving problems they may encounter.

2. **FAQ Page:**

- Create a dedicated Frequently Asked Questions (FAQ) page to address common queries. Organize questions into categories for easy navigation.

3. **Accessing Help Center:**

- Direct users to the Google Sites Help Center for comprehensive documentation and solutions. Provide a link or embed relevant Help Center content to guide users in navigating common challenges.

4. **Common Browser Compatibility Issues:**

- Address browser compatibility issues that users may face. Specify the recommended browsers for optimal performance and provide solutions for common compatibility challenges.

5. **Issues with Page Loading:**

- Troubleshoot issues related to slow page loading. Offer suggestions such as clearing browser cache, checking internet connectivity, or optimizing images for faster loading times.

6. **Login and Access Problems:**

- Provide guidance for users experiencing login or access issues. Include instructions on resetting passwords, checking account permissions, or troubleshooting account-related problems.

7. **Embedding External Content:**

- Address concerns related to embedding external content. Guide users on obtaining correct embed codes, ensuring compatibility, and troubleshooting issues with third-party integrations.

8. **Mobile Responsiveness:**

- Assist users with mobile responsiveness issues. Offer tips on testing the site on various devices, optimizing content for mobile viewing, and ensuring a consistent user experience.

9. **Broken Links and Missing Content:**

- Address concerns about broken links or missing content. Advise users on checking link URLs, verifying file permissions, and troubleshooting issues related to content visibility.

10. **Permissions and Collaboration Issues:**

- Guide users facing problems with permissions or collaboration. Provide instructions on adjusting sharing settings, inviting collaborators, and resolving issues related to collaborative editing.

11. **Version Control and Recovery:**

- Help users understand version control and recovery features. Offer step-by-step instructions on accessing version history, reverting changes, and recovering content.

12. **Customization Challenges:**

- Troubleshoot customization issues users may encounter. Provide solutions for problems related to adjusting layouts, colors, fonts, or other design elements.

13. **SEO and Visibility Concerns:**

- Address questions related to SEO and visibility. Offer tips on optimizing content for search engines, improving page rankings, and enhancing the overall online presence of the site.

14. **Interactive Element Errors:**

• Assist users experiencing errors with interactive elements. Provide troubleshooting steps for issues with embedded media, buttons, forms, or other interactive features.

15. **Social Media Integration Problems:**

• Address challenges related to social media integration. Provide guidance on obtaining and embedding social media feed codes, troubleshooting display issues, and ensuring seamless integration.

16. **Feedback and Support Channels:**

• Encourage users to provide feedback and report issues. Include information on support channels such as contact forms, email addresses, or community forums where users can seek assistance.

17. **Regularly Update FAQs:**

• Regularly update the FAQs section to reflect new questions, changes in site features, or updates to Google Sites. Keep the information current to provide users with accurate troubleshooting guidance.

18. **Encourage User Engagement:**

• Foster a community by encouraging users to share their experiences and solutions. Include a discussion forum or community platform where users can interact, share tips, and support each other.

By addressing common issues and providing clear solutions in your troubleshooting section and FAQs, you empower users to navigate challenges independently and ensure a positive experience with your Google Sites project.

CHAPTER 7

SHOWCASING YOUR TEAM'S WORK

- **Team Pages Creation: Highlighting team members and projects.**

Create compelling team pages on your Google Sites project to showcase team members and highlight ongoing projects. Follow these steps to effectively highlight your team:

1. **Design a Team Page Template:**

- Establish a consistent layout and design for team pages. Include sections for team member profiles, project highlights, and any relevant information about the team.

2. **Individual Team Member Profiles:**

- Feature individual team member profiles on the team page. Include names, roles, brief bios, and professional photos. Provide links to their professional profiles or contact information.

3. **Project Showcases:**

- Showcase current and past projects undertaken by the team. Include project descriptions, key achievements, and visuals such as images, videos, or project-related documents.

4. **Testimonials and Quotes:**

- Incorporate testimonials or quotes from team members regarding their experiences and contributions. This adds a personal touch and highlights the collaborative spirit within the team.

5. **Interactive Elements:**

- Enhance engagement with interactive elements such as clickable images, project timelines, or links to detailed project pages. These elements can provide additional information and context.

6. **Team Achievements Section:**

- Dedicate a section to highlight team achievements, awards, or significant milestones. Celebrate successes to showcase the team's capabilities and expertise.

7. **Collaboration Tools Integration:**

- Integrate collaboration tools directly into the team pages. Embed Google Docs, Sheets, or Slides that demonstrate collaborative work and achievements.

8. **Call-to-Action Buttons:**

- Include call-to-action buttons on team pages. These buttons can lead visitors to contact the team, explore project details, or learn more about individual team members.

9. **Consistent Branding:**

• Maintain consistent branding across team pages. Use the same color scheme, fonts, and design elements to create a cohesive and professional look.

10. **Links to Related Pages:**

• Link team pages to related content within your Google Sites project. Connect team pages to project pages, relevant documents, or external resources for a comprehensive experience.

Google Workspace Collaboration: Enhancing Teamwork with Drive, Docs, and Calendar

Optimize collaboration within your team by seamlessly integrating Google Workspace tools. Enhance teamwork with Google Drive, Docs, and Calendar:

1. **Google Drive Integration:**

• Embed Google Drive folders or documents directly into your Google Sites project. This allows team members to access shared files and resources without leaving the site.

2. **Document Collaboration with Google Docs:**

• Encourage real-time collaboration on documents by embedding Google Docs directly into team pages. Showcase meeting notes, project plans, or collaborative reports.

3. **Google Calendar for Team Events:**

- Embed a shared Google Calendar on team pages to highlight upcoming events, meetings, or project milestones. Ensure that the calendar is accessible to all team members.

4. **Collaborative Editing:**

- Highlight the collaborative editing features of Google Docs and Google Sheets. Illustrate how multiple team members can work on the same document simultaneously, fostering efficient teamwork.

5. **Google Forms for Feedback:**

- Utilize Google Forms for collecting feedback from team members. Embed forms on relevant team pages to gather input on projects, processes, or team dynamics.

6. **Task Management with Google Sheets:**

- Showcase the use of Google Sheets for task management and project tracking. Embed project-related spreadsheets to demonstrate how the team collaboratively manages tasks and timelines.

7. **File Versioning and History:**

- Highlight the versioning and history features in Google Drive. Emphasize how these features support collaboration by allowing team members to track changes and revert to previous versions if needed.

8. **Team Communication with Google Meet:**

• Promote the use of Google Meet for virtual team meetings. Embed links to upcoming or recurring meetings directly on team pages for easy access.

9. **Shared Drive Organization:**

• Illustrate the organization of shared drives within Google Drive. Showcase how folders and files are structured to facilitate easy access and collaboration on shared resources.

10. **Mobile Collaboration:**

• Emphasize the seamless collaboration experience across devices. Showcase how team members can access and collaborate on Google Workspace tools using desktops, tablets, and mobile devices.

User Interaction: Encouraging Feedback and Contact

Foster user interaction on your Google Sites project by encouraging feedback and providing clear contact options. Here's a guide on encouraging user interaction:

1. **Feedback Forms:**

• Create dedicated feedback forms using Google Forms. Embed these forms on relevant pages to collect user opinions, suggestions, or comments about the content and user experience.

2. **Contact Information Section:**

- Include a dedicated section with contact information. Provide an email address, phone number, or other relevant contact details for users to reach out with inquiries or feedback.

3. **Live Chat Integration:**

- Explore live chat integration options. Embed live chat widgets on your site to facilitate real-time communication and address user queries promptly.

4. **Social Media Engagement:**

- Prominently display links to your social media profiles. Encourage users to engage with your content on social platforms and provide feedback or comments.

5. **Comment Sections:**

- Enable comment sections on pages where user interaction is valuable. This allows users to leave comments, ask questions, or engage in discussions related to the content.

6. **Interactive Polls:**

- Use Google Forms to create interactive polls. Embed polls on specific pages to gather user opinions or preferences related to your content.

7. **Newsletter Sign-up:**

•   Include an option for users to subscribe to newsletters or updates. Provide a clear call-to-action and a simple sign-up form to keep users informed about new content or developments.

8. **User Surveys:**

•   Periodically conduct user surveys to gather insights into user preferences, satisfaction, or areas for improvement. Encourage participation by embedding survey links on relevant pages.

9. **Contact Forms:**

•   Create user-friendly contact forms using Google Forms. Embed these forms on pages where users may have specific inquiries or need assistance.

10. **Response and Follow-Up:**

•   Demonstrate responsiveness by promptly responding to user feedback or inquiries. Clearly communicate how users can expect to be contacted and the estimated response time.

11. **Incorporate User Testimonials:**

•   Feature positive user testimonials on your site. Highlighting feedback from satisfied users can build trust and encourage others to engage with your content.

12. **Acknowledgment of Feedback:**

- Acknowledge user feedback and demonstrate its impact on your site. Showcase instances where user input has led to improvements, updates, or additions to your content.

13. **Engaging Calls-to-Action:**

- Incorporate engaging calls-to-action encouraging users to interact. This could include prompts like "Share Your Thoughts," "Join the Conversation," or "Tell Us What You Think."

14. **Moderation of User-Generated Content:**

- If applicable, implement moderation for user-generated content such as comments or forum discussions. Ensure a positive and respectful online community by enforcing clear guidelines.

15. **Accessibility and Inclusivity:**

- Ensure that your site is accessible to a diverse audience. Provide contact options or feedback forms that accommodate users with different needs, including those with disabilities.

By actively encouraging user interaction through feedback mechanisms, contact options, and engaging content, you create a vibrant and inclusive community around your Google Sites project.

- **Achievements Showcase: Highlighting team accomplishments.**

Showcase your team's accomplishments effectively on your Google Sites project with a dedicated Achievements Showcase. Here's how to highlight and celebrate team successes:

1. **Introduction to Achievements Page:**

- Create an introductory section explaining the purpose of the Achievements Showcase. Briefly describe the significance of the showcased accomplishments in the context of your team's goals and mission.

2. **Interactive Display of Achievements:**

- Use visually appealing and interactive elements to display achievements. Incorporate images, videos, or infographics to illustrate key milestones, awards, or successful projects.

3. **Categorize Achievements:**

- Categorize achievements for easy navigation. Create sections or tags based on themes such as projects completed, awards received, milestones reached, or any other relevant criteria.

4. **Project Highlights:**

- Dive deeper into specific projects by providing detailed highlights. Include project descriptions, key challenges overcome, innovative solutions implemented, and the impact of each project on your team or organization.

5.   Awards and Recognitions:

•   Dedicate a section to showcase awards and recognitions received by the team. Include information about the award, the criteria for selection, and any noteworthy details about the achievement.

6.   Client Testimonials:

•   If applicable, feature testimonials from satisfied clients or stakeholders. Highlighting positive feedback adds credibility to your team's achievements and provides real-world validation.

7.   Timeline of Milestones:

•   Create a timeline showcasing the chronological order of significant milestones. This visual representation offers a comprehensive view of your team's progress and growth over time.

8.   Team Member Contributions:

•   Acknowledge individual team member contributions to specific achievements. Highlight key roles and responsibilities, showcasing the collaborative effort that led to success.

9. **Quantifiable Metrics:**

• Incorporate quantifiable metrics wherever possible. Use charts, graphs, or statistics to illustrate the impact of your team's achievements, whether it's increased efficiency, revenue growth, or other measurable outcomes.

10. **Interactive Infographics:**

• Enhance the visual appeal by incorporating interactive infographics. Use tools like Google Drawings to create dynamic visuals that convey complex information in an engaging manner.

11. **Celebratory Quotes:**

• Include celebratory quotes from team members or stakeholders involved in the showcased achievements. These quotes can provide context, emotion, and personal perspectives on the successes.

12. **Behind-the-Scenes Stories:**

• Share behind-the-scenes stories related to specific achievements. Discuss challenges faced, lessons learned, and the team's perseverance in overcoming obstacles, adding depth to the narrative.

13. **Integration with Collaborative Tools:**

- Integrate collaborative tools directly into the Achievements Showcase. Embed Google Docs, Sheets, or Slides that provide additional details, project timelines, or in-depth analyses related to showcased accomplishments.

14. **Recognition of Team Effort:**

- Emphasize the collective effort of the entire team. Showcase how each achievement is a result of collaboration, teamwork, and the combined skills and expertise of your team members.

15. **Call-to-Action for Visitors:**

- Include a call-to-action inviting visitors to learn more about your team's achievements. Provide links to relevant project pages, case studies, or additional resources for those interested in exploring further.

Social Sharing Features: Increasing Visibility Through Social Media

Increase the visibility of your Google Sites project by incorporating social sharing features. Here's a guide on integrating social media sharing elements:

1. **Social Media Sharing Buttons:**

•   Embed social media sharing buttons on relevant pages of your Google Sites project. Include buttons for popular platforms such as Facebook, Twitter, LinkedIn, and others.

2. **Strategic Placement:**

•   Strategically place social media sharing buttons near engaging content, achievements, or important announcements. Ensure that buttons are easily accessible and visible to visitors.

3. **Customizable Share Messages:**

•   Provide customizable share messages when users click on social media sharing buttons. Craft compelling and concise messages that encourage users to share specific content or achievements with their networks.

4. **Shareable Visual Content:**

•   Create visually appealing content that is shareable on social media. Include images, infographics, or videos that convey key messages and can be easily shared across various platforms.

5. **Share Links to Specific Pages:**

•   Enable users to share links to specific pages or achievements within your Google Sites project. Implement shareable links that lead directly to the content users want to highlight.

6. **Social Media Integration Widgets:**

- Explore social media integration widgets that display live feeds or recent posts from your social media profiles. This provides dynamic content and encourages visitors to follow your team on social platforms.

7. **Embed Social Media Feeds:**

- Embed live social media feeds directly into relevant pages. Showcase real-time updates from your team's social media accounts to keep visitors informed and engaged.

8. **Encourage User-Generated Content:**

- Encourage users to share their experiences or thoughts related to your content. Implement features such as comment sections, discussion forums, or user-generated content submissions that can be shared on social media.

9. **Promote Hashtag Usage:**

- Create and promote a unique hashtag associated with your team or projects. Encourage users to use the hashtag when sharing content related to your achievements, allowing you to track and engage with user-generated posts.

10. **Social Media Cross-Promotion:**

- Cross-promote your Google Sites project on your team's social media profiles. Share links to specific pages, achievements, or announcements to drive traffic from social platforms to your site.

11. **Shareable Resources:**

• Provide shareable resources such as downloadable documents, PDFs, or infographics. Include social media sharing options directly within these resources to expand their reach.

12. **Integration with Social Analytics:**

• Implement social analytics tools to track the performance of shared content. Analyze metrics such as engagement, click-through rates, and social media reach to understand the impact of social sharing features.

13. **Social Media Contests or Challenges:**

• Run social media contests or challenges linked to your Google Sites project. Encourage users to share specific achievements or content, offering incentives for participation to boost visibility.

14. **Shareable Event Pages:**

• If your team hosts events, create shareable event pages on your Google Sites project. Include social media sharing options to facilitate promotion and increase event attendance.

15. **Monitor and Respond to Social Shares:**

•	Monitor social shares of your Google Sites content and respond to interactions. Engage with users who share your content, thank them for their support, and actively participate in discussions sparked by shared content.

By incorporating social sharing features, you empower visitors to amplify your team's achievements and content across social media platforms, ultimately expanding your project's visibility and reach.

CHAPTER 8

LAUNCHING AND MAINTAINING YOUR SITE

- **Launch Preparation: Double-checking content and links.**

Before launching your Google Sites project, ensure a seamless experience for visitors by thoroughly checking content and links. Here's a guide for launch preparation:

1. **Content Review:**

- Conduct a comprehensive review of all content on your site. Check for accuracy, relevance, and consistency throughout pages. Update any outdated information and ensure that the content aligns with your team's goals.

2. **Link Verification:**

- Double-check all internal and external links to ensure they are functional. Test each link to verify that it directs visitors to the intended destination. Correct or remove any broken or outdated links.

3. **File and Media Checks:**

•   Verify the functionality of embedded files, images, and media elements. Confirm that files are correctly linked and can be accessed or downloaded without issues. Optimize images for web viewing to enhance loading times.

4. **Consistent Branding:**

•   Ensure consistent branding across all pages. Check that colors, fonts, logos, and other design elements adhere to your team's brand guidelines. A cohesive visual identity enhances the professionalism of your site.

5. **Spelling and Grammar:**

•   Proofread all content to catch any spelling or grammar errors. Use tools like spell checkers to identify and correct mistakes. Clear and error-free content contributes to a positive user experience.

6. **Accessibility Compliance:**

•   Validate that your site complies with accessibility standards. Ensure that text is readable, images have alternative text, and navigation is intuitive for users with different abilities. Consider running an accessibility audit using online tools.

7. **Browser Compatibility:**

•   Test your site across different browsers (e.g., Chrome, Firefox, Safari, Edge) to ensure compatibility. Address any layout or functionality issues that may arise in specific browsers to provide a consistent experience for all users.

8. **Mobile Responsiveness:**

•   Confirm that your site is fully responsive on various devices, including smartphones and tablets. Test different screen sizes to guarantee that content is easily accessible and displays correctly on all devices.

9. **Forms and Interaction:**

•   Test any forms or interactive elements on your site. Verify that form submissions are received, and interactive features function as intended. Address any issues related to user input and engagement.

10. **SEO Optimization:**

•   Ensure your site is optimized for search engines. Check page titles, meta descriptions, and keywords to improve visibility on search engine results pages. Use SEO tools to analyze and enhance your site's search engine performance.

Testing for Compatibility: Ensuring Responsiveness Across Devices

Guarantee a seamless user experience by thoroughly testing your Google Sites project for compatibility across various devices. Here's a guide for testing compatibility:

1. **Desktop Testing:**

- Test your site extensively on desktop devices, including different screen sizes and resolutions. Ensure that all elements are well-aligned, images load properly, and interactive features function as expected.

2. **Mobile Device Testing:**

- Use various mobile devices (smartphones and tablets) to test your site's responsiveness. Check for readability, navigation ease, and overall layout consistency. Address any issues that may arise on smaller screens.

3. **Tablet Device Testing:**

- Test your site on tablet devices to verify that content adapts appropriately to the screen size. Confirm that navigation is user-friendly and interactive elements respond accurately.

4. **Cross-Browser Testing:**

- Conduct cross-browser testing to ensure compatibility with different web browsers such as Chrome, Firefox,

Safari, and Edge. Resolve any layout or functionality discrepancies that may arise in specific browsers.

5. **Operating System Compatibility:**

• Consider testing your site on different operating systems (Windows, macOS, Linux) to ensure compatibility. Confirm that users on various operating systems have a consistent and positive experience.

6. **Browser Version Compatibility:**

• Test your site on different versions of each browser to ensure compatibility with older and newer releases. Address any issues that may arise due to variations in browser versions.

7. **Navigation and Interactivity:**

• Verify that navigation is intuitive and interactive features work seamlessly across all tested devices. Address any issues related to dropdown menus, buttons, or other interactive elements that may behave differently on various platforms.

8. **Loading Times:**

• Assess loading times on different devices and connections. Optimize images, files, and content to ensure quick loading, especially on mobile networks. Faster loading times contribute to a positive user experience.

9. **Form Submissions:**

- Test form submissions on different devices to confirm that users can submit information successfully. Verify that form data is received accurately and that users receive confirmation messages or emails.

10. **Media Playback:**

- Check the playback of media elements (images, videos, audio) on different devices. Confirm that media files load properly and that users can play them without disruptions.

11. **Cross-Device Consistency:**

- Ensure a consistent user experience across all tested devices. Users should have a similar experience in terms of content accessibility, design, and functionality, regardless of the device they are using.

12. **User Authentication:**

- If your site involves user authentication, test the login and registration processes on various devices. Confirm that users can access secured sections and that account-related features work seamlessly.

Launch Plan Creation: Strategizing for a Successful Website Debut

Prepare for a successful launch of your Google Sites project by creating a comprehensive launch plan. Here's a guide for strategizing your website debut:

1. **Define Launch Goals:**

• Clearly define the goals and objectives of your website launch. Whether it's increasing visibility, attracting users, or promoting specific content, having clear goals will guide your launch strategy.

2. **Target Audience Identification:**

• Identify your target audience and tailor your launch plan to reach them effectively. Understand the demographics, preferences, and behaviors of your audience to create targeted promotional strategies.

3. **Launch Date Selection:**

• Choose a strategic launch date that aligns with your goals and targets your audience effectively. Consider factors such as industry events, holidays, or other relevant occasions for maximum impact.

4. **Pre-Launch Teasers:**

- Generate anticipation by creating pre-launch teasers. Use social media, email newsletters, or other communication channels to offer sneak peeks, behind-the-scenes looks, or countdowns to build excitement.

5. **Social Media Campaigns:**

- Develop a comprehensive social media campaign for your launch. Utilize platforms like Twitter, Facebook, LinkedIn, and Instagram to share engaging content, teasers, and announcements leading up to the launch.

6. **Email Marketing Strategy:**

- Implement an email marketing strategy to reach your existing audience. Send out newsletters, announcements, or exclusive content to subscribers, encouraging them to explore the new site.

7. **Press Release Preparation:**

- Draft a compelling press release highlighting key features, achievements, or unique aspects of your Google Sites project. Distribute the press release to relevant media outlets to secure coverage.

8. **Collaborate with Influencers:**

- Identify influencers or thought leaders in your industry and collaborate with them for your launch. Leverage their reach and credibility to extend the visibility of your project to a broader audience.

9. **Launch Event or Webinar:**

- Consider hosting a virtual launch event or webinar to engage your audience. Use this opportunity to showcase key features, provide demonstrations, and interact with users in real-time.

10. **Community Engagement:**

- Engage with your online community in forums, groups, or discussion platforms related to your industry. Share information about your upcoming launch, answer questions, and build excitement within these communities.

11. **Website Announcements:**

- Create announcements on your current website or other online platforms to inform existing users about the upcoming launch. Include details about new features, improvements, or content they can expect.

12. **User Training Materials:**

- If your Google Sites project introduces new features or functionalities, prepare user training materials. Create tutorials, guides, or videos to help users navigate and make the most of the new site.

13. **Feedback Channels:**

- Establish channels for user feedback immediately after launch. Encourage users to share their thoughts, report any issues, or provide suggestions. Actively monitor these channels to address user input promptly.

14. **Performance Monitoring:**

- Implement tools for monitoring the performance of your site post-launch. Track metrics such as website traffic, user engagement, and conversion rates to assess the impact of your launch strategy.

15. **Post-Launch Celebrations:**

- Celebrate the successful launch of your Google Sites project. Acknowledge the efforts of your team, express gratitude to users for their support, and highlight any immediate successes or positive feedback received.

By carefully planning and executing your launch strategy, you can maximize the impact of your Google Sites project and ensure a positive reception from your target audience.

- **Promotion Strategies: Using social media, email, and networking.**

Effectively promote your Google Sites project using a combination of social media, email, and networking strategies. Here's a guide for promoting your project:

1. **Social Media Campaigns:**

- Develop targeted social media campaigns across platforms such as Facebook, Twitter, LinkedIn, and Instagram. Create visually engaging posts, share project highlights, and use relevant hashtags to increase visibility.

2. **Teasers and Countdowns:**

- Generate excitement by posting teasers and countdowns on social media platforms. Use intriguing visuals, share snippets of content, and build anticipation leading up to the official launch of your Google Sites project.

3. **Shareable Content:**

- Create shareable content that resonates with your target audience. This could include infographics, videos, or blog posts related to the content on your site. Encourage users to share this content within their networks.

4. Engage with Influencers:

- Identify influencers or thought leaders in your industry and engage with them on social media. Share your project with them, ask for their feedback, and seek their support in promoting your Google Sites project to their followers.

5. Social Media Contests:

- Organize social media contests or challenges related to your project. Encourage users to share their experiences, insights, or creations, incorporating specific project-related hashtags. Offer incentives to boost participation and engagement.

6. Live Q&A Sessions:

- Host live Q&A sessions on social media platforms to interact directly with your audience. Answer questions about your project, share behind-the-scenes insights, and address any inquiries or concerns.

7. Collaborative Content:

- Collaborate with other individuals or organizations in your industry. Create joint content, cross-promote each other's projects, or participate in collaborative events to expand your reach.

8. **Email Newsletters:**

•   Leverage your email subscriber list to share updates about your Google Sites project. Craft engaging newsletters that highlight key features, achievements, and recent content additions. Include calls-to-action to drive traffic to your site.

9. **Personalized Email Invitations:**

•   Personally invite key contacts, clients, or stakeholders via email to explore your Google Sites project. Tailor your invitations to highlight elements that may be particularly relevant or interesting to each recipient.

10. **Networking Events:**

•   Attend relevant virtual or in-person networking events within your industry. Share information about your Google Sites project during discussions, presentations, or networking sessions to create awareness among professionals in your field.

11. **Cross-Promotion with Partners:**

•   Identify potential partners or collaborators and explore opportunities for cross-promotion. Share each other's projects, co-host events, or exchange promotional efforts to tap into each other's audiences.

12. **Community Engagement:**

• Engage with online communities and forums related to your industry or niche. Share valuable insights, participate in discussions, and subtly introduce your Google Sites project where appropriate.

13. **Targeted Ad Campaigns:**

• Consider running targeted advertising campaigns on platforms like Google Ads or social media. Create ads that highlight key aspects of your project and target specific demographics to maximize impact.

14. **Interactive Webinars:**

• Host interactive webinars related to your Google Sites project. Share insights, demonstrate features, and engage with participants. Promote these webinars across your social media channels and email newsletters.

15. **Feedback and Testimonials:**

• Encourage users to provide feedback and testimonials about their experience with your Google Sites project. Share positive feedback on your social media and website to build credibility and attract new users.

Regular Maintenance: Updating Content and Performing Backups

Ensure the ongoing success of your Google Sites project by implementing regular maintenance practices. Here's a guide for updating content and performing backups:

1. **Content Review Schedule:**

• Establish a regular schedule for reviewing and updating content on your Google Sites project. This could be weekly, bi-weekly, or monthly, depending on the frequency of changes and updates within your team.

2. **Update Announcements:**

• Inform users about content updates through announcements on your site. Create a dedicated section or banner to highlight recent changes, additions, or important announcements, keeping users informed and engaged.

3. **Content Relevance Assessment:**

• Regularly assess the relevance of existing content. Identify outdated information, obsolete resources, or content that may need refreshing. Update or remove content to ensure accuracy and usefulness.

4. **Scheduled Backup Routine:**

• Implement a scheduled routine for backing up your Google Sites project. Use Google Drive or other cloud storage solutions to create regular backups of your site's content, ensuring data security and the ability to restore if needed.

5. **Media and File Checks:**

• Check the functionality of embedded media, files, and links regularly. Ensure that images load correctly, files are accessible, and all linked content remains functional. Address any issues promptly to maintain a seamless user experience.

6. **Security Updates:**

• Stay informed about security updates related to Google Sites. Regularly check for platform updates or security patches and apply them promptly to protect your site and its users from potential vulnerabilities.

7. **Performance Optimization:**

• Optimize your site's performance regularly. Evaluate loading times, address any issues affecting speed, and optimize images or media files to maintain a fast and efficient user experience.

8. **User Feedback Monitoring:**

•   Actively monitor user feedback channels for any comments, suggestions, or reported issues. Use this feedback to make informed decisions about updates, improvements, or additional features based on user needs.

9. **Collaborative Tool Updates:**

•   If your site integrates with collaborative tools such as Google Drive or Google Calendar, stay informed about updates to these tools. Ensure that your site remains compatible with the latest features and functionalities.

10. **Browser Compatibility Checks:**

•   Periodically conduct browser compatibility checks. Test your site on different browsers and versions to identify and address any compatibility issues that may arise due to browser updates.

11. **Mobile Responsiveness Assessment:**

•   Regularly assess the mobile responsiveness of your site. Test it on various devices to confirm that content displays correctly and that users on smartphones and tablets have a positive experience.

12. Feedback Implementation:

- Act on user feedback by implementing necessary changes and improvements. Use feedback as a valuable resource for refining your site's content, features, and overall user experience.

13. Community Engagement:

- Continue engaging with your online community and industry forums. Stay connected with your audience, participate in discussions, and gather insights that can inform future updates to your Google Sites project.

14. Training Material Updates:

- If your project involves training materials or user guides, keep them up-to-date. Update tutorials, guides, or videos to reflect any changes to the site's features, layout, or functionalities.

15. Regular Site Audits:

- Conduct regular site audits to assess overall performance, functionality, and user experience. Identify areas for improvement, address any emerging issues, and ensure that your Google Sites project aligns with your team's evolving goals.

By consistently updating content, performing backups, and staying proactive in maintenance efforts, you can keep your Google Sites project fresh, secure, and aligned with the evolving needs of your users and team.

CONCLUSION

Congratulations on completing the journey of creating and launching your Google Sites project! In this comprehensive guide, you've explored every aspect of building a website, showcasing your team's work, and fostering effective collaboration. Let's recap the key takeaways:

1. **Foundational Knowledge:**

- You've gained a solid understanding of the basics of Google Sites, from its fundamental features to its advantages in creating websites and collaborating seamlessly.

2. **Step-by-Step Guide:**

- The guide provided a step-by-step approach, starting with account setup and defining the purpose of your website. You've learned how to structure content, customize design elements, and make your site accessible to a wide audience.

3. **Collaboration and Multimedia:**

- Emphasizing collaboration, you explored real-time editing, multimedia insertion, and collaborative features that enhance teamwork on projects. The guide detailed how to manage team access, integrate Google Workspace, and ensure version control.

4.   **Advanced Features and Optimization:**

- As you progressed, the guide delved into advanced layout options, external tools integration, and optimizing your site for search engines. Interactive elements and social media integration were covered to engage visitors and boost visibility.

5.   **Troubleshooting and FAQs:**

- A dedicated section addressed common issues and provided solutions. This ensures a smooth user experience and addresses potential challenges users may encounter.

6.   **Team Pages, Google Workspacc Collaboration, and User Interaction:**

- You learned to create team pages, enhance collaboration with Google Workspace tools, and encourage user interaction. These strategies foster a vibrant and inclusive community around your Google Sites project.

7.   **Achievements Showcase and Social Sharing Features:**

- Highlighting team accomplishments and incorporating social sharing features amplifies the impact of your project. These elements contribute to building credibility, expanding visibility, and encouraging user engagement.

8. Launch Preparation and Testing:

• The guide outlined meticulous launch preparation, testing for compatibility across devices, and creating a launch plan. These steps ensure a successful debut of your Google Sites project.

9. Promotion Strategies and Regular Maintenance:

• Strategies for promoting your project through social media, email, and networking were explored. Additionally, regular maintenance practices, including content updates and backups, were emphasized to sustain your site's success over time.

In conclusion, your journey doesn't end with the launch; it's a continuous process of refining, promoting, and maintaining your Google Sites project. Keep engaging with your audience, adapting to evolving needs, and celebrating the achievements of your team. Your website is a dynamic tool for collaboration, communication, and showcasing the excellence of your work. Best of luck on your continued journey with Google Sites!

www.ingramcontent.com/pod-product-compliance
Lightning Source LLC
Chambersburg PA
CBHW070530160726
48003CB00004B/1749